It was time for art class.

Kim sat next to Jeff.

"Let's paint our pets!" said Jeff.

Jeff painted his cat.

Kim painted her dog.

My Cat

Kim looked at Jeff's painting.
"That looks like a dog!" said Kim.

Jeff looked at Kim's painting.

"That looks like a cat!" said Jeff.

Jeff changed the name of his painting.
So did Kim.

8